The Whooping Crane

The Whooping Crane

A COMEBACK STORY

By Dorothy Hinshaw Patent

Photographs by William Muñoz

CLARION BOOKS

TICKNOR & FIELDS: A HOUGHTON MIFFLIN COMPANY

NEW YORK

ACKNOWLEDGMENTS

The author and photographer wish to thank the following people for their help with the project: David Ellis, Rod Drewien, Wendy Brown, Janet McMillan, Kathy O'Malley, Scott Derrickson, Ernie Kuyt, the late Frank Johnson, Tom Stehn, Ted Appell, Phil Norton, Ed Merritt, and Rob Horwich.

The painting on page 13 is reproduced courtesy of the Metropolitan Museum of Art, Gift of Harry G. C. Packard and Purchase, Fletcher, Rogers, Harris Brisbane Dick and Louis V. Bell Funds, Joseph Pulitzer Bequest and The Annenberg Fund, Inc. Gift 1975. The photos on pages 20, 21, 22, and 40 are supplied by the Canadian Wildlife Service and used with their permission. The photo on page 56 is by David Ellis. The photo on page 63 is by Rod Drewien.

Clarion Books
Ticknor & Fields, a Houghton Mifflin Company
Text copyright © 1988 by Dorothy Hinshaw Patent
Photographs copyright © 1988 by William Muñoz

Book design by Sylvia Frezzolini
Printed in the U.S.A.

P   10   9   8   7   6   5   4   3   2   1

LIBRARY OF CONGRESS CATALOGING-IN-PUBLICATION DATA

Patent, Dorothy Hinshaw.
    The whooping crane.

    Includes index.

    SUMMARY: Traces the forty-year-old and ongoing attempt to save the endangered whooping crane from extinction, focusing on efforts at wildlife refuges and the captive breeding program.
    1. Whooping cranes—Juvenile literature.   2. Rare birds—Juvenile literature.   3. Birds, Protection of—Juvenile literature.   [1. Whooping cranes.   2. Rare birds.   3. Birds—Protection.   4. Wildlife conservation.]
I. Muñoz, William, ill.   II. Title.
QL696.G84P38   1988   639.9′7831   88-2871
ISBN 0-89919-455-9

To the memory of Frank Johnson,
with thanks to Ted and his angels

CONTENTS

ONE   The Magnificent Whooper   9

TWO   Winter in the South   27

THREE   Scientists Help the Whooper   39

FOUR   Creating a New Flock   59

FIVE   The Future of the Whooping Crane   73

            Index   85

CHAPTER ONE

The Magnificent Whooper

The elegant whooping crane is the tallest bird in North America, reaching five feet in height. A seven-foot wing-span makes the flying whooping crane a magnificent sight, its snow-white body contrasting boldly with jet-black wingtips. When a whooping crane, or whooper, is on the ground, the black feathers are hidden. Then the bird looks pure white, except for black facial markings and a bright red patch of bare skin on the top of its head.

In the 1940s, the whooping crane almost disappeared. Since the first European settlers came to North America over 300 years ago, we have lost many living treasures through the careless activities of humans. Birds, which are especially appealing and noticeable, have been among the most spectacular losses. The passenger pigeon, for example, dwindled in number from billions to zero in less than a hundred years. Close calls with other animals have been numerous, and conservationists are working hard to rescue many endangered species from extinction. But perhaps the most remarkable ongoing rescue is that of the whooping crane.

THE CRANE FAMILY

The whooper belongs to a small family of large, powerful birds, all called cranes. Only 15 kinds, or *species,* of cranes exist. They inhabit every continent except South America and Antarctica. Like the whooper, other cranes have long legs and necks. They have powerful pointed beaks and unwebbed feet. Most species have colorful skin patches on the head. Males and females look alike, although the males are usually slightly larger. Both parents help care for the one to four young. Some species, such as the sandhill crane, are very numerous. Other kinds besides the whooper are considered endangered, including the red-crowned and Siberian cranes.

Wherever they have lived, these unique birds have impressed humans since ancient times. Their large size, graceful "dancing," and powerful voices set them apart from most other birds. Cranes were painted on the walls of Egyptian tombs 3,000 years ago. Some letters of the Greek alphabet are said to have been based on the formations of cranes in flight.

Cranes mate for life, and in China and Japan, they are

The crowned crane lives over much of Africa and is commonly seen in zoos in America.

Hooded cranes breed in the USSR and spend the winter in Japan,
Korea, and China.

This Japanese
hanging scroll
painted in the
early 1700s is
typical of Asian
art featuring
cranes. (The
Metropolitan
Museum of Art,
The Harry G.C.
Packard
Collection
of Asian Art)

13

used in wedding designs as symbols of longevity and happiness. Chinese art sometimes shows the soul of a dead person riding to heaven on the back of a crane.

In Japan, the crane has developed a new meaning in recent times. In the mid-1950s, a young Japanese girl named Sadako Sasaki lay dying of leukemia caused by radiation from the Hiroshima atomic bomb blast. Because it was said that making a thousand paper cranes would bring long life, she tried her hardest to reach that lucky number, folding paper crane after crane. She died after creating 644. Nowadays August 6 is Peace Day in Japan. On that day, children lay colorful chains of handmade paper cranes sent from all over the world beneath Sadako's statue in the Hiroshima Peace Park as symbols of peace.

Becoming Endangered

The whooping crane (known to science as *Grus americana*), like so many other American animals, became a victim of the rapid expansion of the United States and Canada as settlers moved west. The original range of the whoopers stretched from the Arctic coast to central Mexico and from Utah to New Jersey. The cranes wintered in southern states such as Louisiana, Texas, and South Carolina and bred in Minnesota, Iowa, Illinois, North Dakota, and northward into Canada. Some birds in Louisiana did not migrate but stayed in the same area year-round. But by 1894, whooping cranes no longer nested anywhere in

the northern United States. Hundreds had been shot for food and for their decorative feathers. In addition, many of their breeding marshes had been destroyed as wetlands were drained to make room for towns and farmland.

The whooper population was never very large. Even before European settlement, there were probably no more than 5,000 birds, and by the mid-1800s, around 1,300 remained. From then on, it was all downhill for the whoopers. They reached a population low in 1941, with 15 birds wintering in Texas and six in Louisiana. The Louisiana birds soon vanished, leaving only a tiny remnant of whooping cranes in the world.

From a dangerously small population, the whooping crane has now reached far more promising numbers. In early 1988, about 150 lived in the wild and 42 in captivity. How has the success so far been accomplished? Ingenuity and creative management by experts in Canada, Maryland, Texas, New Mexico, and Idaho have combined to make the future of the whooper look hopeful, although not yet secure.

WHERE DO WHOOPERS NEST?

The first crucial chapter in the story of the whooper's comeback begins with the search for the birds' nesting area. The Aransas National Wildlife Refuge on the Gulf Coast of Texas was established in 1937 to protect whoopers on their wintering grounds. But saving the small remnant population required knowing where the birds went in the spring to breed. From Aransas, the whoopers flew north over Oklahoma, Kansas, Nebraska, and the Dakotas, disappearing as they continued north over Saskatchewan. Somewhere in the wilderness of Canada, far from the sight of humans, the whoopers were secretly building nests and raising chicks. But where?

The hunt for the nesting grounds began in 1945. For three years, the Canadian wilderness was searched by air,

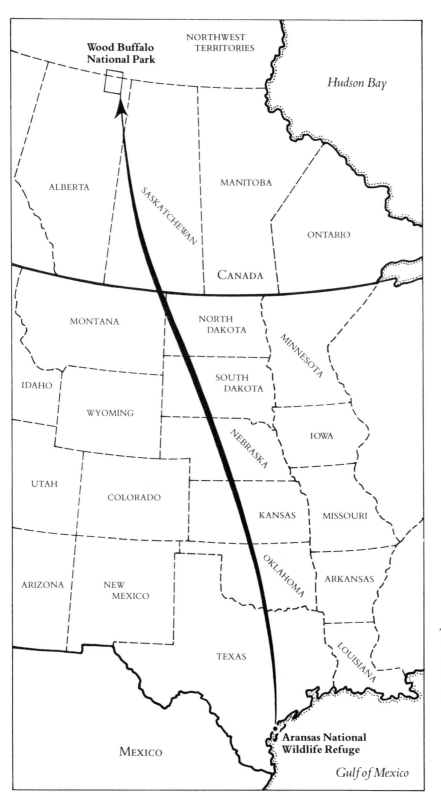

The Flight
Path of the
Whooping
Cranes

all the way north to the Arctic Coast, with no success. After the formal searches were suspended, wildlife biologists still hoped to find the whoopers' summer home. People along the flight path were asked to look out for whoopers on the wing and to keep from disturbing them.

Finally, in 1954, a helicopter pilot patrolling near a fire in Wood Buffalo National Park in the Northwest Territories of Canada spotted a pair of big, white birds with a fluffy, young chick—unmistakably whooping cranes. The nesting grounds had been found purely by accident. Biologists were relieved that the birds were raising their precious offspring within the boundaries of a national park; they were already protected from human disturbance. The region had been searched from the air before without anyone spotting the birds, which shows how well the whoopers had chosen their remote home.

The inaccessibility of the nesting area explains why these few whoopers survived while all others perished. It is so swampy that it is even difficult for a helicopter to touch down, and the open water areas are too small for a floatplane to land nearby. There are no rivers passable by canoe. People came nowhere near, and predators like wolves were somewhat deterred by the water.

RAISING A FAMILY

The whooping cranes arrive at their nesting grounds during late April or early May. Although the northland is still frigid then, the days are rapidly getting longer. When

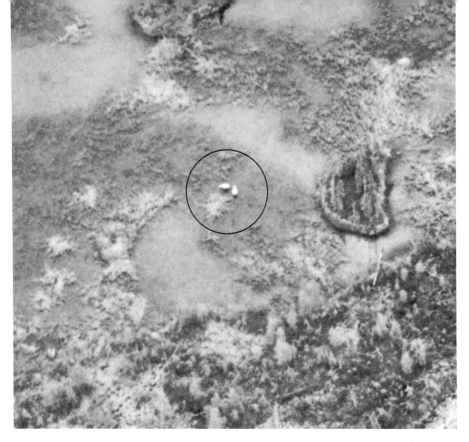

This photo, taken from an airplane, shows the very marshy area where whooping cranes breed. Notice the pair of cranes near the center of the picture.

spring arrives, it comes with a burst of life. Each whooper pair soon builds a three-foot-tall mound out of bulrush and other plants. The nests are in shallow ponds and extend about 15 inches above the water. Each family needs a large area, called its territory, which the adults defend against other whoopers and potential enemies. The nests are usually at least eight-tenths of a mile apart. If they are closer, the parents may be less successful in raising their family.

A whooping crane nest with two eggs.

Each female lays one or two eggs, and the pair takes turns incubating them for about 30 days. Every day, the parents carefully turn the eggs, which helps keep the developing chicks from sticking to the shells.

When the eggs hatch, the wet chicks are covered with downy, tan feathers. Their eyes are open, and they can walk soon after they are dry. Although two eggs may be laid, only one chick normally survives to fledging, the stage it is able to fly. This fact may seem sad but, as we will see, it has turned out to be crucial in the whooper rescue effort. For the first two or three days, the chicks need to be kept warm

Whooper parent with a chick at far left.

much of the time. But then the family leaves the nest and spends the summer wandering through its territory, feeding on insects, berries, and other foods.

The parents devote their attention to their fluffy offspring, feeding the chicks and protecting them from danger. A young whooper grows rapidly and can fly by the time it is about two-and-a-half months old. After the baby down is lost, the first coat of feathers is a rusty cinnamon color, completely different from the pure white and black plumage of the adult. By the time it can fly, the

This young captive whooper will be old enough to fly by
September.

baby is almost as tall as its parents. It already possesses the elegant beauty of a crane, but it still has the soft look of a baby, with its fluffy neck and head feathers and its soft gray-blue eyes. When it opens its mouth, instead of a triumphant whoop, it gives out the peeping whistle of a baby bird.

Heading South

In the fall, the whooper families head south. The parents stay with their chick, guiding it along the perilous 2,400 mile journey until the birds reach Aransas National Wildlife Refuge in late October or November. Because the birds travel in small family groups, it is difficult to determine their flight path. But knowing where they stop to rest is critical in order to protect them along the route.

In 1981, Canadian and American biologists attached radio transmitters to bands on the legs of whooping crane chicks. The transmitters were powered by batteries and solar cells. They were very light in weight and did not interfere with the birds' ability to fly. A pilot in a small plane fitted with radio antennas on each wing followed a whooper family in flight. When the birds stopped to rest, biologists on the ground were alerted to their position and carefully noted the characteristics of the resting place.

Four families were followed for at least part of their southward migration during 1981 and 1982. One family took just 31 days to make the journey, traveling on 17 of these days and resting and feeding on 14. They tended to spend time in the grainfields of southern Saskatchewan. There they tanked up on grain to fuel their long flight until bad weather forced them on. Along the trip south, the birds stopped wherever they could find a suitable place at the end of a day's flight. Sometimes they rested at wildlife refuges, but more often they landed on private farms with ponds and grainfields. Thus, the cranes must depend on the cooperation of private citizens as well as wildlife managers to protect them.

White pelicans are among the birds that share the Aransas refuge
with the whoopers.

Winter in the South

The Texas Gulf Coast is a haven for water birds. Herons, gulls, pelicans, and about 300 other bird species share the Aransas refuge and the offshore islands with the whooping cranes. The land is very flat. Wind and tide carry seawater into shallow ponds surrounded by coarse, salt-tolerant plants. These pools provide protected feeding areas for the whoopers. The warm, shallow waters also harbor a variety of fish, crabs, clams, and other food, and grainfields provide further nourishment. While most cranes feed largely on grain, whooping cranes also eat large quantities of crabs, clams, acorns, and berries.

FAMILY HOMES

Each whooper family defends its own territory in winter as well as in summer. A pair returns to the same territory

A pair of whoopers looks for food at Aransas.

year after year. In the fall, after arriving on the wintering grounds, the birds may squabble over the boundaries of their territories. But soon things settle into a routine, with each family staying within its own area. Subadult birds (those under the usual mating age of five or more) do not defend a territory and try to squeeze into areas defended by adult cranes. Adult males keep a lookout for invaders and challenge them with a loud whooping cry. During such a confrontation, the bird's mate joins in. If the intruders refuse to leave, the male may fly toward them, protesting loudly as he comes. This usually convinces the other birds to depart.

The male's role in maintaining a territory is important. When a female with a chick returned one fall without her mate, she was unable to defend a territory on her own. The two birds were soon homeless. Luckily for her, however, a nearby male had also lost his mate. She moved into his territory, and the two partial families teamed up. Officials at the refuge nicknamed the new family "the Brady bunch" after a TV show about a man with children marrying a woman who also has children. Together, the two adult whoopers managed to raise their chicks through the winter.

A whooper chick with one of its parents in February. Notice the rust-colored feathers on its head and tail.

While both parents care for and protect the chick, the mother does most of the feeding. The chick is already almost as tall as its parents, but its cinnamon color sets it clearly apart. When the family arrives at Aransas, the chick already has white feathers on its wings and is getting some white body feathers, too. As the winter progresses, white feathers continue to replace the juvenile plumage. By March, only a few rust-colored feathers on the head distinguish the youngster from its parents.

The young bird gradually learns to feed itself as well, and the parents let it wander more and more as time goes by. By February, the young bird can find most of its food on its own. In the weeks before leaving, the parents may at times actually chase their offspring away. Soon, the chick will have to care for itself. By the time the birds return to Canada to breed, the young whooper will be on its own.

When the whooping crane population was at its low, each family had a very large winter feeding territory of 400 to 600 acres. Wildlife biologists wondered what would happen as the number of birds grew. When Aransas was established, 80% of the cranes lived within its boundaries during the winter. How many whooping cranes could live on the refuge? As they bred successfully, would they drift away and settle on unprotected lands?

Fortunately, established pairs made room for new ones as the population increased. Families now have smaller territories (about 300 acres) than they did before. But

A family together on its territory at Aransas. The parent with the chick is probably the mother, while the one on the lookout is most likely the father.

some pairs have also set up homes on nearby Matagorda Island and on Saint Joseph's Island. Fortunately, two-thirds of Matagorda Island is part of the refuge. The owner of Saint Joseph's Island also cooperates in protecting the cranes.

COMMUNICATING WITH ONE ANOTHER

The whooper's spectacular calls are among its most impressive traits. While all cranes make loud sounds, the whooping crane's is perhaps the most penetrating. It may be heard at a distance of well over a mile. The crane's windpipe, or *trachea,* is long and curved. It is held in place by a groove in the breastbone. Species that make the loudest sounds have the longest, most looped windpipes. The trachea's extra length aids in producing the characteristic calls. The whooper's trachea is about 58 inches long, the same length as the bird itself.

When a whooper pair is defending its territory, the birds join together in a *unison call.* The male points his beak skyward and emits a penetrating trumpeting sound. The female follows with two higher, shorter notes. This coordinated duet is repeated over and over. When whoopers are two or three years old and starting to pair up, they begin to vocalize the typical notes of the unison call even when in a group. Occasionally, young birds may give out the call of the opposite sex. But the unison call can be used to accurately determine the sex of adult cranes.

One reason humans are so attracted to cranes is their beautiful "dancing." Whoopers may dance at any season. But as departure time from Texas comes closer, the male and female spend increasing amounts of time carrying out this graceful display. Often, only part of the dance is performed.

A complete dance begins with one bird bowing its head and flapping its wings, then leaping into the air with stiffened legs while throwing its head to the sky. The other bird responds by running toward its mate while bobbing its head up and down, wings aflap. Then both

A pair of captive whoopers give the unison call.

If an intruder does not leave, the whooper pair continues to display, raising their feathers and arching their necks so that the red patches on the tops of their heads face forward.

The dances of different crane species are similar. Here a pair of
sandhill cranes perform.

birds jump up and down together with their legs stiff and their necks arched upward. The jumping may be interrupted when the birds run toward each other while bowing their heads and stretching out their wings, followed by more wild leaping. The dancing may continue for several minutes, with elegant bows alternating with agile leaps.

TIME TO TAKE OFF

In March and April, the whoopers get more and more restless. All they need now is the strong southeast wind typical of this time of year to help carry them northward, and they will be on their way. When the moment arrives, they stretch out their necks and lean into the wind like statues. Then they spread their great wings and lift off, circling skyward on the updraft until they are just visible as distant specks heading north.

For the adult cranes, the spring migration is more hurried than the fall trip, taking a total of only two to five weeks. It is important for them to arrive on the breeding grounds in plenty of time to prepare a nest, incubate their eggs, and raise a chick big and strong enough for the return flight in September. Whoopers usually fly at an altitude of 1,000 to 2,000 feet, taking advantage of the wind currents when possible, but they may go as high as 13,000 feet above sea level.

CHAPTER THREE

Scientists Help the Whooper

By 1960, the Texas-Canadian whooper population, which was only 15 in 1941, had increased to 36. But these few birds still could have been wiped out by disease or natural disaster. Concern about the fate of this beautiful bird led to studies and discussions of the best way to secure its future.

Because a wild pair of whooping cranes often produces two eggs but almost never raises more than one chick, conservationists felt that the second egg could be removed without affecting the recovery of the wild crane population. In 1964, the Canadian Wildlife Service and the U.S. Fish and Wildlife Service signed an agreement to allow whooping crane eggs to be removed from nests in Wood Buffalo National Park to be hatched in captivity.

CRANES IN CAPTIVITY

In 1967, scientists began taking one egg from each nest with two eggs and carefully transporting the eggs to the Patuxent Wildlife Research Center in Laurel, Maryland. Since then, many whooping cranes have been raised successfully at Patuxent. By 1987, 44 precious whoopers were living there.

The Patuxent scientists work with a number of other endangered birds, including the Mississippi sandhill crane. The sandhill crane (*Grus canadensis*) has six subspecies, which look slightly different from one another. Besides the Mississippi race, there are the Florida, Cuban, Canadian, greater, and lesser sandhill cranes.

Scientists often use the greater sandhill crane, which is not endangered, to test methods for raising other cranes in captivity. They began studies on incubation of crane eggs and hand rearing of the chicks six years before the first whooper eggs were removed from nests at Wood Buffalo.

Whooper eggs in their nest at Wood Buffalo National Park. One of them is beginning to hatch.

In that way, they had confidence in their procedures before they began to raise endangered crane species. Even so, some techniques had to be modified once the scientists began working with the less adaptable whoopers. For example, whooping crane chicks can develop leg abnormalities under some conditions in captivity if their diet and exercise are not carefully controlled.

Several different methods are now used in raising cranes at Patuxent. Fortunately, the same basic techniques that work for sandhills are effective with whoopers as well. Each mated crane pair lives in its own large pen, with food and water available at all times. Whooping cranes feed mostly on animal food in the wild, but in captivity they do well on the same food pellets as sandhills.

The crane pens are carefully built to keep out predators. Two strands of electrified wire run along the fence. One is near the ground and the other is near the top. Any animal that tries to climb the fence will get an unpleasant shock. The fencing material is also buried well into the ground to discourage burrowers.

Cranes chosen as potential foster parents for endangered cranes must undergo an evaluation process lasting several years before being given the responsibility of raising a whooper. Whooper eggs and young whooper chicks look almost exactly like their sandhill counterparts, and sandhill parents will readily take care of them as if they were their own. Whoopers also will accept sandhill eggs and chicks in the same way.

A whooping crane at Patuxent approaches its food inside a protected shed in its pen.

TOP: The cranes are provided with constantly running fresh water.
BOTTOM: Five immature whoopers share a pen at Patuxent.

ABOVE: An adult whooping crane.   BELOW: An adult sandhill crane.

A crane pair is first given a greater or Florida sandhill egg. If the foster parents raise the chick successfully, they are given nonendangered sandhill eggs for three more seasons. If they prove to be consistently good parents, they may be trusted with endangered Mississippi sandhill eggs and chicks for the next three years. Success with that bird puts them in line as possible foster parents for a precious whooper.

The behavior of every pair is carefully monitored. Most good parents do well throughout incubation and rearing of the chicks. But some are great incubators and poor at raising chicks. Others may be careless about proper incubation but may take especially good care of chicks. If one of these latter pairs will raise a whooper, it is first provided with a sandhill egg to incubate. Just before the egg is ready to hatch, a whooper egg is substituted into the nest. The adults do not notice the change and carefully raise the whooper chick that hatches.

EXTRA-SPECIAL CARE

Not all the eggs are incubated by crane foster parents. Often, those of the endangered birds are incubated indoors, where conditions can be better controlled. Special machines keep the eggs at a constant temperature of 99.5° F and at the proper humidity. The eggs are on racks that rotate automatically every two hours, and they are inspected once a day. After 30 days, the eggs are ready to hatch. They are moved to a hatcher, which is slightly

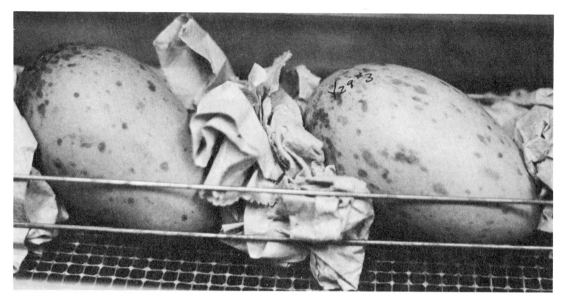

Two sandhill eggs in an incubator. The numbers indicate which female laid the eggs and whether it was her first, second, and so forth.

cooler than the in cubator and has higher humidity. Once the egg hatches, the chick is carefully tended. It is weighed and it gets a dose of antibiotic every day for the first three days.

Mechanical incubators are not the only alternative to lying in the nest under a warm crane. Sandhill crane eggs have been successfully incubated by a golden eagle, and large chickens are being tried as crane incubators. Because the eggs are so big, however, the hen cannot turn them herself. A human has to shoo her off the nest twice a day to do the job.

This newly hatched Mississippi sandhill weighed in at 116 grams, about one-fourth pound.

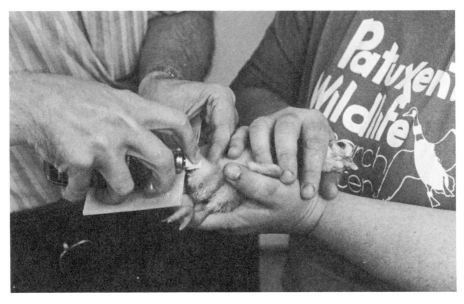

After being weighed, the new chick got a protective antibiotic spray on its still-wet umbilical cord.

Hand-rearing problems

While some Mississippi sandhill and whooping crane chicks are raised by foster parents, others are carefully brought up in protected indoor pens. But hand-rearing by humans presents problems for cranes. Like many other birds, cranes identify with whatever creature acts as a parent to them. This process is called *imprinting*. In nature, imprinting allows young birds to develop a strong attachment to their natural parents. It enables them to learn what to look for when they grow up and are ready to mate. But for captive-raised cranes, imprinting can cause great confusion, for birds can imprint on people instead of on their own kind.

Perhaps the best-known case of such imprinting involved a female whooping crane named Tex. Tex lived at the International Crane Foundation in Baraboo, Wisconsin. Scientists there wanted her to breed. But Tex was strongly imprinted on people, and the Foundation had no male whoopers anyway. Director George Archibald was determined not to waste Tex's potential to produce priceless offspring, so he decided to take the role of her mate. He lived with her for weeks and danced with her when she wanted to dance. The gamble paid off. When Tex was ready to mate, she was *artificially inseminated*—whooper sperm sent to Baraboo from Patuxent was introduced into her reproductive tract by Dr. Archibald. The result was an egg that later hatched.

Not only do hand-reared cranes sometimes refuse to

A sandhill crane chick looks almost identical to a whooper chick. The band on its wing holds an identification number.

pair with an appropriate mate, they also look upon all humans as equals and defend their territories against their caretakers. If a human enters the pen of a whooper raised by people, the bird behaves toward the person as it would toward another crane. Instead of running away, the crane shows threat behavior. Such cranes may even attack humans. Being stabbed by a crane's powerful beak is not a pleasant experience. When entering a pen harboring hand-reared cranes, workers may have to use brooms to hold off the birds while doing their chores.

IMPRINTING ON CRANES

Scientists are now developing ways of raising young cranes that will make it difficult for them to imprint on people. At Baraboo, keepers are experimenting with wearing a crane costume when caring for sandhill chicks. In that way, the cranes can be carefully tended without getting accustomed to seeing human beings. If this method works, it could be used with whooping cranes as well.

At Patuxent, some sandhills and whoopers are raised in carefully planned environments to help them imprint as cranes. A stuffed *brooder model* is placed in the pen. The model has raised wings, and a heat lamp above provides a heat source. The chicks can seek protection and warmth near the crane model, just as they would under a parent in the wild. The head and neck of a dead crane are mounted and suspended above the food dish so that the chicks will

At the International Crane Foundation, Rob Horwich wears a crane suit with a bright red head to help a young sandhill imprint as a crane.

Young Florida sandhills in their indoor pen. The brooder model is at the left. Notice the turkey chick to the left of the sandhills.

associate being fed with the head of an adult crane. Wild crane parents feed their young by holding morsels in their beaks, which the babies then take. Keepers also use this model to feed the chicks. The model's beak is dipped into water and then into crumbled chicken feed, which sticks to it. The young cranes peck the food off the beak.

Chicken or turkey chicks are added to the crane "family," too. They show the cranes where the food is and also act as targets for crane aggression. Instead of pecking at another valuable crane, a chick will aim its aggression at the chicken or turkey instead. A live adult crane of the same species is kept in the pen next door. Plexiglas protects the chicks from attack by the adult bird, but they can still see it and will associate themselves with that bird.

When whooping cranes are raised this way, white whooperlike models are made from other species. The brooder model is constructed from the bodies of two dead snow geese attached to legs of a sandhill. The feeding model is a sandhill crane head bleached with human hair dye. Next door lives a sandhill that has been bleached to look white. Its head is carefully marked with black and red paint to make it look like a whooper. Scientists hope that these methods will allow the young cranes to grow up identifying with their own kind.

Crane chicks can be aggressive to one another. Here the chick on the left challenges the other, then chases after it.

A sandhill's head is carefully colored to resemble a whooper. This bird lived in its own pen between two whooper chicks. Scientists hope that this will help the chicks recognize themselves as whooping cranes.

GETTING MORE EGGS

By 1975, whoopers raised at Patuxent were old enough to lay eggs themselves. The scientists also developed a method for getting more than two eggs from the females each season. Artificial lights turned on in the winter fool the cranes' bodies into thinking that springtime has come. The females are ready to mate in March or early April, over a month earlier than birds in the wild. They are then artificially inseminated until they are ready to lay. After the first egg is laid, it is taken away. The bird is insemi-nated again so that the second egg is also fertile. In ten days to two weeks, the bird lays again and the egg is removed. This process is continued through the spring-time until the bird has laid as many as eleven eggs. Thus, each female crane in captivity can be much more produc-tive than one in the wild.

The Patuxent workers hope that captive whoopers will mate successfully without artificial insemination in the near future. Some young birds that have already chosen mates will be left alone to see if they can produce fertile eggs on their own. If they can, it will be one more step in the effort to allow captive whoopers to live as naturally as possible.

A captive whooper chick spreads its wings.

CHAPTER FOUR

Creating a New Flock

By 1975, 57 whoopers were counted in the wild flock that annually took the lengthy journey from Aransas to Wood Buffalo and back. At Patuxent, the first whooper had begun to lay eggs. The existence of the captive cranes insured that the species could continue even if disaster hit the wild population. But no one could rest easy until another wild population of the cranes could be established. How to do it? With no other wild whoopers to show the way, how could birds somehow placed in the wild learn where to nest, how to migrate, and even where to go?

STARTING THE FLOCK

Some years earlier, scientists had the idea that perhaps sandhill cranes could nurture and teach young whoopers the secrets of successful living in the wild. Could wild sandhills be tricked into taking care of young whoopers? If so, then perhaps a new flock of whoopers could slowly be built in association with sandhills.

With this idea in mind, Dr. Roderick Drewien of the University of Idaho had been studying a sandhill flock that nested at Grays Lake National Wildlife Refuge in Idaho. Over the years, he had banded many sandhills so their movements could be traced. Most of the flock migrates only about 850 miles to its wintering grounds in the

Sandhill cranes.

Middle Rio Grande Valley of New Mexico. Along the way the birds stop to rest in the San Luis Valley of Colorado. National wildlife refuges—Bosque del Apache in New Mexico and Alamosa and Montevista in Colorado—provide protection for the migrating cranes. During most of their lives, these birds are relatively well protected from the dangerous world created by humans.

In 1975, the U.S. Fish and Wildlife Service and the Canadian Wildlife Service began an exciting experiment. At the end of May, 14 whooper eggs were removed from two-egg nests in Canada and flown to Idaho. There they were substituted for sandhill eggs in the nests of carefully selected birds. Those chosen were consistently successful parents that tended to keep away from roads and other signs of human activity. The scientists hoped that by picking such foster parents for the precious whoopers, the endangered birds would have the best chance for survival. The sandhill eggs removed from the nests were shipped to Patuxent, where they were incubated and the chicks were raised.

Worries and Concerns

During that exciting first season, the scientists had plenty to worry about. Would the sandhills accept the whooper chicks? Would they continue to do so when the chicks grew rust and white feathers instead of the typical gray and rust plumage of young sandhills? How would the young whoopers respond to the normal wild sandhill diet?

As-young chicks, both species are fed insects and other small animal food, but after leaving the nesting grounds, sandhill food consists mostly of grain.

Fortunately, wild sandhills proved to be excellent parents for their rather different foster chicks. The lovely rust-colored young were accepted by all the sandhills. Some whoopers survived and grew well on the more vegetarian diet of their adoptive parents. Altogether, four chicks made it through the perilous stages of infancy that first year.

Since then, more whooper chicks have been raised by sandhills at Grays Lake. Many of the whoopers have died. But by early 1988, about 20 whoopers lived with the sandhills along the Rio Grande during the winter. Most of the birds spend the winter at Bosque del Apache. But some settle north of the preserve, and others travel farther south into Mexico. In the spring, they all head north. Many do not return to Grays Lake. The yearling whoopers tend to wander. Older males, however, do fly back to Grays Lake, where they set up territories when they are two or three years old. The older females are likely to scatter to new areas in the summer. In 1986, some female whoopers from the flock traveled to Montana and Wyoming instead of going to Grays Lake. In 1987, one female spent the summer all alone in a remote part of Yellowstone National Park. Scientists are trying to figure out the best way to get these whoopers to pair up and mate.

The question of mating is crucial. At the beginning of

Wendy Brown releases a whooper chick after banding it. All the whooper chicks at Grays Lake are given bands with radio transmitters so they can be easily tracked.

the foster parent program, some scientists feared the whoopers might grow up identifying with sandhills. Then they might try to pair with them rather than with their own kind and would never produce a new generation of whoopers. If the whoopers mated successfully with sand-

A whooper feeds among the sandhills in the San Luis Valley of Colorado.

hills, problems could be created by the resulting hybrid birds. Luckily, the mating rituals and calls of the two species are quite different, so scientists thought it unlikely that the whoopers could successfully establish pairs with the sandhills.

To see what would happen if the two species mated, a female sandhill at Patuxent was artificially inseminated with sperm from a whooper male. This allowed scientists to find out if hybrids could be produced. They could also get an idea of what the hybrids looked like so they could be recognized and removed from the wild if necessary. The odd-looking "whoophills" that hatched from the hybrid eggs were very different from either parent. Scientists were relieved when the one that reached adulthood proved to be infertile. Today, the whoophill lives on at Patuxent. He has a greater sandhill crane for his mate, and the two of them are excellent foster parents. One day, this pair may be allowed the honor of raising a whooping crane chick.

The male whoophill and his sandhill mate are good foster parents to the sandhill chick they are raising.

Managing the Cranes

Almost 300 other bird species share Bosque del Apache with the cranes, along with hundreds of kinds of mammals, reptiles, and amphibians. The refuge must be carefully managed to protect all the wildlife, but special attention goes to the endangered whoopers. Grain is grown and cut down to provide plenty of winter food for the cranes and other birds, such as snow geese. Biologists keep a close watch on the cranes in case problems develop.

Snow geese follow behind as grain is cut at Bosque del Apache. The grain feeds cranes as well as the geese.

Bosque del Apache National Wildlife Refuge is a haven
for many birds, including cranes.

Tens of thousands of snow geese came to Bosque del Apache in
1986.

Hunters who want to hunt snow geese at Bosque del Apache must pass a training course in bird identification so they can recognize whoopers and other protected birds. They are allowed to use only steel shot in their shotguns. Many birds, including whooping cranes, mistake lead shot for the gravel or grit they normally consume. As a result, the birds can die from lead poisoning. This is a serious problem not only for cranes but also for ducks and geese and the eagles that may feed on their bodies after they die. Steel shot, on the other hand, is harmless to birds that eat it.

These management methods, along with others such as regulating the water flow into ponds the birds use to roost and feed, help keep the refuge a safe and healthy home for the precious whoopers.

A U.S. Fish and Wildlife Service employee at Bosque del Apache checks hunters' shotgun shells with a magnet to make sure they contain steel rather than lead shot.

The Future of
the Whooping Crane

By early 1988, the world whooper population had grown from 21 in 1941 to a total of perhaps 195—132 in the Wood Buffalo flock, about 20 in the Grays Lake population, 41 at Patuxent, 1 at the San Antonio Zoo, and 1 at the International Crane Foundation in Wisconsin. These numbers are very encouraging. But natural disasters could still kill off large numbers of whoopers, so no one breathes easily yet about the fate of the whooping crane.

DANGERS AND PERILS

The birds still face many perils, and some whoopers are lost each year to natural and human causes. Cranes collide with power lines or fences and die. Hunters may mistake whoopers for sandhill cranes or snow geese and shoot them. Stormy weather during migration and disease are always potentially deadly to the cranes. Since whooping cranes do not begin to produce offspring until they are about five years old and even then raise no more than one chick a year, it would take a long time to recover from any large population loss.

Unfavorable conditions in Wood Buffalo can also cause problems. In 1981, the breeding grounds were very dry, and only two of the ten chicks that hatched survived to

reach Aransas. The lack of water probably made it easier for predators to capture the chicks. Fortunately, many more young usually survive. In 1987, 25 of the 27 chicks that hatched lived to fly south toward Texas. This was a new record.

The only wild breeding flock also faces dangers in Texas. The birds could be wiped out in one major disaster such as a late, fierce hurricane or an oil spill. Barges carrying dangerous chemicals frequently pass through the

Coyotes are predators of cranes, especially young chicks.

A whooping crane feeds along the shore at Aransas. It walks slowly
along the water's edge and plunges its head into the water to grab
a clam or crab with its strong, sharp beak.

waterway. One poisonous spill near the wintering grounds could kill most of the birds. The fact that a few whoopers now winter off the refuge reduces the risk of a total catastrophe. But wildlife biologists worry that harm could come to birds living away from the protection offered by the refuge.

PROTECTING WILD WHOOPERS

Education is one way to keep some of the dangers to wild cranes at a minimum. The government and the National Audubon society print flyers showing how to recognize whoopers in flight so that hunters will not shoot them. Thousands of people visit Bosque del Apache and Aransas each year and learn about how they can help protect these great birds.

At Bosque del Apache, avian cholera and tuberculosis are two diseases that can be passed from one kind of bird to another. If the snow goose population is high, the danger of an epidemic increases. When hunters bag snow geese there, they must bring the birds to a refuge check station where employees remove the internal organs to check for disease. In that way, managers can be forewarned about a possible epidemic that could imperil the whoopers.

Power lines can also be dealt with. The most dangerous wire is the thin static line that runs highest on the poles. When weather causes poor visibility, the birds may not see this wire, and wind can also blow them against it. In

A farmer in the San Luis Valley near Alamosa, Colorado, has painted a silo in celebration of the great whooper.

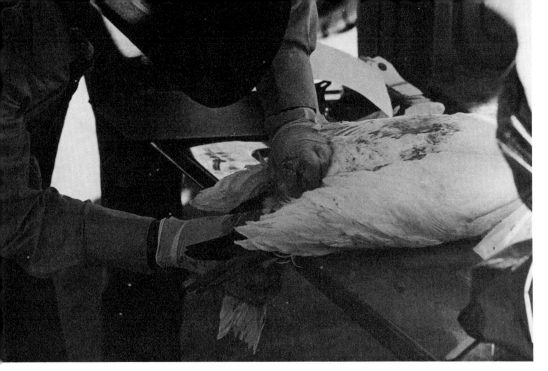

A U.S. Fish and Wildlife Service employee removes the internal organs of a snow goose shot by a hunter at Bosque del Apache; they will be sent to a laboratory to check for disease.

Sandhills fly over power lines. The static line that runs across the tops of the poles is the most dangerous to cranes.

one area in which many sandhill cranes kept hitting a static line and dying, the line was removed. This can be done only in a few areas, for the static wire protects the power lines from lightning strikes, but there are other ways of protecting birds from this danger. In Japan, power lines have been marked with plastic streamers so cranes can more easily avoid them. Crane biologists and power company officials in areas where whoopers live are now experimenting with marking lines that pass through areas frequented by cranes.

SECURING THE FUTURE
Conservationists will not rest until the future of the whooping crane is more secure. This will require several

advances, including setting up another captive breeding program so that an epidemic or other disaster at Patuxent will not wipe out the captive population. The number of breeding pairs at Wood Buffalo should increase to 40 from the 1987 total of 32 in order to provide a buffer for losses from disease or disaster. Scientists estimate that the winter habitat around Aransas could comfortably accommodate that many birds along with their offspring and the non-breeding subadults. If all goes well, this number will be reached sometime in the 1990s.

Two more wild populations that breed successfully should also be established. The Grays Lake birds have not yet mated, so it isn't clear whether this exciting experiment will prove to be a success in terms of perpetuating

As the cranes in the Grays Lake population get older, the chances of a male and female pairing up and producing young increases.

the whooping crane. Scientists hope that with time, the birds will form pairs and produce whooper chicks. The male whoopers return to Grays Lake for the summer, but the female birds tend to wander. The females will be caught and taken to Grays Lake for the breeding season in 1988. That way, the females will be near the males, increasing the chances that they will pair up. If the Grays Lake whoopers do not breed, the whole idea of using wild sandhills as foster parents will need to be reevaluated.

Meanwhile, officials are discussing where and how to establish a third wild whooper flock. The upper peninsula of Michigan, the Okefenokee swamp in Georgia, and several sites in Florida are being carefully evaluated as homes for whoopers. Another area of Canada could also be in the running. There is a distinct advantage of choosing a southern location, however. The flock would be nonmigratory, like the Louisiana population that died out in the early 1940s. Since the birds would stay in the same area all year round, they would face fewer dangers and could be more easily monitored. They could also be released as young birds, about six months old, instead of being raised by wild sandhills. Captive-bred Mississippi sandhills have already been successfully released in this way. By 1995, whoopers will probably be living again in the wild somewhere east of the Mississippi River, and their thrilling cries will again be heard on the wind.

Page numbers in *italics* refer to captions.

Alamosa National Wildlife Refuge, 61

Aransas National Wildlife Refuge, 16, 27–31, 75, 77

Archibald, George, 48

artificial insemination, 48, 56–57

Bosque del Apache National Wildlife Refuge, 61, 62, 67, *67, 68, 70,* 77, *79*

brooder model, 50, *52,* 53

Canada, 14, 16–19; *see also* Wood Buffalo National Park

coyote, *75*

cranes, 10–14, 27

chicks, *47, 49, 54, 55*

crowned, *11*

foster parents, 41–44, *66*

greater sandhill, 40

hand-rearing, 48–53

hooded, *12*

incubation of eggs, 45–46

Mississippi sandhill, 40, 45, *47,* 48, 83

red-crowned, 10

Siberian, 10

symbolism of, 10–14

traits of, 10

see also sandhill crane, whooping crane

diseases of birds, 77, *79*
Drewien, Roderick, 60

Florida, 83

Grays Lake National Wildlife Refuge, 60, 62, *63,* 81–83

hunting, 71, 73–74

Illinois, 14
imprinting, 48, 50–53
International Crane Foundation, 48, 50, *51*
Iowa, 14

Japan, *12,* 14

Louisiana, 14, 16, 83

Matagorda Island, 31
Mexico, 14, 62
Michigan, 83
Minnesota, 14
Montevista National Wildlife Refuge, 61

New Jersey, 14
North Dakota, 14

Okefenokee swamp, 83

paper cranes, 14
passenger pigeon, 9–10
Patuxent Wildlife Research Center, 40–57, *42, 43, 46, 47, 52, 56, 58,* 61
Peace Day, 14
pelican, white, *26*
power lines, 73, 77–80, *79*

Saint Joseph's Island, 31
sandhill crane, *35,* 40, *44, 49, 60, 64, 75*
  as foster parents, 41–44, 59–65
  food of, 41, 62
Sasaki, Sadako, 14
shotgun shot, 71
snow geese, *67, 70,* 71, 77, *79*
South Carolina, 14

Tex, 48
Texas, 14; *see also* Aransas National Wildlife Refuge
trachea, 32

Utah, 14

whoophill, 66, *66*
whooping cranes
  captive breeding, 39–57

chicks, 21–24, *22, 29,* 30, *31, 58*

color of, 9, 21, 22, 23

communication by, 31–36

dancing, 32–36

dangers to, 73–77

eggs, 21, 39–41, *40,* 56–57

endangered status, 14–16

food, 22, 27, 41, 62, *76*

future of, 80–83

migration of, 16–19, 24–25, 36, 62

nesting, 19–21

population size, 15–16, 39, 59, 73

range, 14

size of, 9

subadults, 28

territories of, 20, 27–29, 30–31

unison call, 32, *33*

voice, 31–32

Wood Buffalo National Park, *18,* 19–24, 39, 74–75, 81

ABOUT THE AUTHOR

Dorothy Hinshaw Patent was born in Minnesota and grew up in Marin County, California. She received a Ph.D. in zoology from the University of California at Berkeley. She and her author/husband Gregory now live in Missoula, Montana. They have two grown sons. Dr. Patent has written more than thirty-five books for children and young adults, most of which have been selected as Outstanding Science Trade Books for Children. Two of her books received awards from the Society of Children's Book Writers, and one, *Spider Magic,* was an American Library Association Notable Book for 1982. Most recently, Dr. Patent received the 1987 Eva L. Gordon Award for Children's Science Literature given by the American Nature Study Society in recognition of her many outstanding books for young readers.

ABOUT THE PHOTOGRAPHER

William Muñoz, a freelance photographer, has collaborated with Dr. Patent on many of her books. He received a B.A. in history from the University of Montana. He, his wife Sandy, and their young son Sean live on a farm near St. Ignatius, Montana. Mr. Muñoz traveled to Aransas National Wildlife Refuge in Texas and Bosque del Apache National Wildlife Refuge in New Mexico to photograph whooping cranes in the wild. He also traveled to the Patuxent Wildlife Research Center in Maryland where many whoopers are being successfully bred in captivity. At Grays Lake National Wildlife Refuge in Idaho, Mr. Muñoz took photos of the whoopers being raised by sandhill cranes in the wild.